DRILL & THRILL

DRILL & THRILL

Fun, Fast Ways to Review Almost Anything

LAUREEN REYNOLDS

Crystal Springs
BOOKS
A division of SDE Staff Development for EDUCATORS.

Peterborough, New Hampshire 03458

Published by Crystal Springs Books
A division of Staff Development for Educators (SDE)
10 Sharon Road, PO Box 500
Peterborough, NH 03458
1-800-321-0401
www.crystalsprings.com
www.sde.com

Published 2008
Printed in the United States of America
12 11 10 09 08 1 2 3 4 5

ISBN: 978-1-934026-13-7

Editor: Kristy Erickson
Art Director and Designer: Soosen Dunholter
Production Coordinator: Deborah Fredericks
Illustrator: Mary Ruzicka

Contents

INTRODUCTION 8

KOOSH BALL BLAST..9
Content suggestions: Skip counting (2s, 5s, 10s, 25s, 50s, 100s, 1,000s), traditional counting (with random starting points), alphabet sequence, months of the year, days of the week

COWBOYS & CHICKENS....................................10
Content suggestions: High-frequency words, fluency phrases, math facts, spelling words, vocabulary words, shapes (simple and complex), place value identification (write the place you want students to identify/read aloud in a different color)

FOLLOWING FOOTPRINTS................................12
Content suggestions: High-frequency words, math facts, vocabulary words, coin identification (front and back), number recognition (to 1,000), word families

SPOTLIGHT...14
Content suggestions: Numbers on a number line, high-frequency words, sounds/symbols on an alphabet line, geographic locations, shapes (simple and complex), science information on posters (plant structure, for example)

BEANBAG BOCCI **16**

Content suggestions: Time, geographic locations (use a map instead of preparing a grid), high-frequency words, number recognition (to 1,000), coin identification (front and back), coin combination totals, vocabulary words, math facts, blend/digraph sounds, shapes (simple and complex), colors

ROLL, READ & REPEAT **17**

Content suggestions: Coin identification (front and back), high-frequency words, shapes (simple and complex), number recognition (to 1,000), letter recognition, blend/digraph sounds, word families

STAND UP, SIT DOWN..**18**

Content suggestions: Parts of speech, number sense, math facts, word families, shapes (simple and complex), coin identification (front and back)

OVER YOUR HEAD **20**

Content suggestions: Coin identification (front and back), number recognition (to 1,000), high-frequency words, colors, shapes (simple and complex), fraction pieces, fluency phrases

RING MY BELL..**22**

Content suggestions: Compound words, greater than/less than, synonyms, parts of speech, correct spelling

BEACH BALL BONANZA..**23**
Content suggestions: High-frequency words, math facts, letters, letter sounds, number recognition (to 1,000), shapes (simple and complex)

KINGS & QUEENS **24**
Content suggestions: High-frequency words, spelling words, math facts, number recognition (to 1,000), coin identification (front and back), shapes (simple and complex), colors

LIGHTS, CAMERAS, ACTION..**26**
Content suggestions: High-frequency words, math facts, number recognition (to 1,000), shapes (simple and complex), coin identification (front and back), word families, fluency phrases

SAY WHAT? **28**
Content suggestions: Spelling words, math facts, high-frequency words, letter recognition, word families

BOOM WHACKERS **29**
Content suggestions: Spelling words, skip counting (2s, 5s, 10s, 25s, 50s, 100s, 1,000s), math facts, backward counting, syllable counting, months of the year, days of the week, alphabet sequence

LAND HO! **30**
Content suggestions: High-frequency words, word families, blend/digraph sounds, number recognition (to 1,000), shapes (simple and complex), colors, coin identification (front and back), math facts

Introduction

I created *Drill & Thrill* because, as a primary teacher, I couldn't bear to review skills in the traditional "drill-and-kill" format: flash cards. It was not only boring but also ineffective. Recent research tells us that we need to get children's bodies involved in our instruction and connect pictures and colors to the information we want them to remember. *Drill & Thrill* does that and more.

Each activity in this book contains a quick, fresh, interactive method for reviewing words, phonics rules, math concepts, or other content that can be done *in less than five minutes*. All of the activities can be used for more than one kind of review, and each one is designed to engage your students' bodies and brains in novel ways.

On each page you will find the title of the drill, a list of necessary materials (items you most likely already have), content information that would be most appropriate to use with the drill, and how to do it. Each activity also contains one or more variations you may want to incorporate into your drill rotation.

Using this quick reference will turn your "drill and kill" into "drill and *thrill*." Have fun!

Koosh Ball Blast

MATERIALS
◆ Koosh ball

CONTENT SUGGESTIONS
Skip counting (2s, 5s, 10s, 25s, 50s, 100s, 1,000s), traditional counting (with random starting points), alphabet sequence, months of the year, days of the week

HOW TO DO IT
Have students sit in front of you on the floor, slightly spread out so they cannot touch one another. Announce what you will be reviewing (counting by 2s, for example) and begin the sequence by saying "Two." Toss the ball to a student, who continues the sequence ("Four") and then tosses it back to you. Continue the sequence ("Six"), then toss the ball to another student, who says "Eight" and tosses it back to you. Continue until everyone has had a turn or until you reach a predetermined number, then start over.

VARIATIONS
Using a different kind of soft "ball" each time you do this is fun. Try a tennis ball, a dog's chew toy, a rolled-up pair of socks, or items from students' personal collections. Older students may enjoy the challenge of you providing half of an information pair while they provide the other half. One example would be state capitals: you say "New York," and the student responds with "Albany."

Cowboys & Chickens

MATERIALS
- Marker
- 4 x 6-inch index cards
- Glue
- Individual pictures of cowboys and chickens (computer generated or hand-drawn)

CONTENT SUGGESTIONS
High-frequency words, fluency phrases, math facts, spelling words, vocabulary words, shapes (simple and complex), place value identification (write the place you want students to identify/read aloud in a different color)

HOW TO DO IT
Write the information you want to review on index cards. On a few cards, glue a picture of a cowboy or a chicken and intersperse the pictures with the cards containing the information you're reviewing. Gather students on the floor in front of you. If you show them a word, for example, have them read it out loud.
If you show them a picture of a cowboy, have them yell "Yee ha!"
If you show them a picture of a chicken, have them yell "Bock, bock!"

VARIATIONS

Change the pictures to correspond with each month's theme to mix things up a bit. Have students help you decide what the pictures/noises should be. Older students may enjoy using pictures of snowboarders ("Dude!") and tarantulas ("Eek!").

Following Footprints

MATERIALS
- ◆ Pencil
- ◆ Construction paper
- ◆ Scissors
- ◆ Thick erasable marker
- ◆ Duct tape

CONTENT SUGGESTIONS
High-frequency words, math facts, vocabulary words, coin identification (front and back), number recognition (to 1,000), word families

---

HOW TO DO IT

Using the pencil, trace your footprints on construction paper. Cut them out and laminate them. Make as many pairs of footprints as you need for your focus content. Using the marker, write your focus information on the footprints. Tape the footprints to the classroom or hallway floor (a change of venue is great for the brain) in a left-right format. Line students up single file at the beginning of the trail. The first student in line reads the first footprint, steps on it, reads the second one, steps on it, and continues until he comes to the end. (At this point, he can encourage his classmates from the sidelines or go to the end of the line for another turn.) When the first student is about one-quarter of the way along the trail, the second student starts. Then the third student, the fourth student, and so on, until everyone has had the number of turns you desire. When you are finished using the footprints, have students help you erase them so the footprints will be ready for the next set of focus information.

VARIATION

You may write something on each footprint that requires students to give you a related answer. For instance, if you write "I will" on a footprint, students must say the contraction for those words when they step on it.

Spotlight

MATERIALS	**CONTENT SUGGESTIONS**
◆ Large, bright flashlight	*Numbers on a number line, high-frequency words, sounds/symbols on an alphabet line, geographic locations, shapes (simple and complex), science information on posters (plant structure, for example)*

HOW TO DO IT

Turn the lights off in your classroom and pull the blinds if possible. Shine the flashlight on a number on your number line and say "Ready, set, spotlight," to which students respond verbally with the number. Move to another number, repeat the phrase, and have students respond with the number. Shining your light first and using the phrase gives students that find-and-think time that is so valuable to ensure their participation and success. Be sure to focus on only one concept during each spotlight session to maximize the effectiveness of your drill time.

VARIATIONS

Ask students to bring their own flashlights from home. After you say "Ready, set, spotlight," they too can shine their lights on the number and then say it. You may also allow students to take turns being the "spotlighter." If you are drilling numbers or letters in particular, you can make it more challenging by asking students to respond with the number or letter that comes before or after the one you have spotlighted.

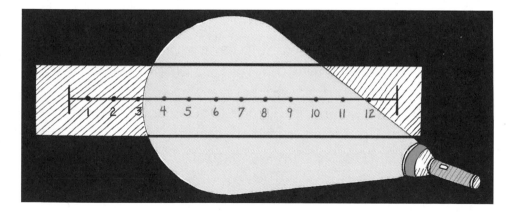

Beanbag Bocci

MATERIALS
♦ Marker
♦ 3 x 5-inch index cards
♦ Poster board grid (with 9, 12, or 16 boxes) for each group
♦ tape
♦ Beanbag for each group

CONTENT SUGGESTIONS
Time, geographic locations (use a map instead of preparing a grid), high-frequency words, number recognition (to 1,000), coin identification (front and back), coin combination totals, vocabulary words, math facts, blend/digraph sounds, shapes (simple and complex), colors

HOW TO DO IT
Write the information you want to review on index cards. Make one set of cards for each grid. To prepare each grid, tape one card inside each box. (Your students can help you with this.) Divide students into small groups and give each group a beanbag. In turn, each student tosses the beanbag onto the grid and names the word, math fact, shape, etc., that the beanbag lands on. The rest of the group can repeat what the player said, then begin a new turn. You can reuse the grids by removing the index cards.

VARIATION
Older students may enjoy having a competition. Give each student a checklist of the items on the grid. Students check off each item as they land on it. The first student to complete her checklist wins.

Roll, Read & Repeat

MATERIALS
◆ Masking tape

◆ One or two large foam dice or wooden blocks for each group (You can make these out of poster board as well.)

◆ Marker

CONTENT SUGGESTIONS
Coin identification (front and back), high-frequency words, shapes (simple and complex), number recognition (to 1,000), letter recognition, blend/ digraph sounds, word families

HOW TO DO IT
Place one piece of masking tape on each side of each die and write your focus information on the pieces of tape. Divide students into small groups. Give each group one 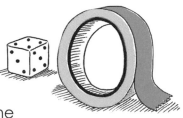 or two dice. The first child rolls the die (or dice) and identifies the word, number, etc., that appears. The rest of the group repeats what the roller said. If the groups are using two dice, students should read and repeat the information on one die at a time. Students then take turns rolling the die or dice until everyone has a turn.

VARIATION
Students can make a list of the words (or other content) that appear on the die or dice before starting and make predictions about which ones will come up most often. A recorder or secretary in each group makes a tally mark next to each word each time it is rolled. The group can check their predictions at the end of the drill.

Stand Up, Sit Down

MATERIALS
♦ Marker

♦ 4 x 6-inch index cards

CONTENT SUGGESTIONS
Parts of speech, number sense, math facts, word families, shapes (simple and complex), coin identification (front and back)

HOW TO DO IT

Students can sit in their chairs for this drill, but you may want them to move away from their desks a bit. The drill requires students to apply a skill, not just repeat the information in front of them. Write your content of choice on index cards. Tell students what the criterion for this drill is. If you are focusing on parts of speech, the criterion might be "The word is a verb." Hold up each index card. If the word on the card is a verb, students stand up and sit back down as quickly as possible. If it is not a verb, they stay seated. If you are focusing on number sense, the criterion might be "The number is greater than 57." If the number on the card is greater than 57, students stand up and sit down quickly. If not, they remain seated.

VARIATION

If you are drilling verbs or nouns, you can use pictures instead of words. Hold up the card, name the picture, and wait for your students' response. This makes the information more accessible to more students and is a great differentiation technique.

Over Your Head

MATERIALS
♦ Overhead materials that reflect content (Remember, anything that can be placed on the photocopier glass can be copied onto a transparency, so you do not need specially made overhead materials.)

CONTENT SUGGESTIONS
Coin identification (front and back), number recognition (to 1,000), high-frequency words, colors, shapes (simple and complex), fraction pieces, fluency phrases

HOW TO DO IT
This drill follows traditional "drill-and-kill" format, but the use of the overhead and corresponding materials makes it much more interesting, because you can add color, pictures, and novel objects to the mix. Place a transparency featuring a coin, number, word, etc., on the overhead glass. Ask students to identify it and then say "That's not over our heads!" Repeat the process as time allows.

VARIATION

To make this even more interesting, let students lie on the floor. Flip your overhead's mirror up to project the content onto the ceiling.

Ring My Bell

MATERIALS
- Marker
- 4 x 6-inch index cards
- Jingle bells for each student

CONTENT SUGGESTIONS
Compound words, greater than/less than, synonyms, parts of speech, correct spelling

HOW TO DO IT

This is another criterion-based drill. Write the content that is appropriate for your class on index cards. Give each student a bell. During this drill, students ring their bells if what you show and say to them fits the criterion established. If your focus  is on compound words, your criterion might be "The word is a compound word." Read the word as you show the index card. If the word is "football," for example, students ring their bells, because "football" is a compound word. If the word is "hockey," the bells should remain silent. Remember to scaffold students with any necessary skill reminders before and during this drill.

VARIATIONS

You can include a picture on each index card to make things more interesting. If you want students to respond to items that do not fit the criterion as well, allow them to decide on and use a sound that they can make with their mouths, such as a buzzer noise or a gong ringing.

Beach Ball Bonanza

MATERIALS
- Beach ball
- Permanent marker

CONTENT SUGGESTIONS
High-frequency words, math facts, letters, letter sounds, number recognition (to 1,000), shapes (simple and complex)

HOW TO DO IT

Blow up the beach ball and write your focus content on it. If you choose math facts, be sure to include the answer. (If you do not include the answer, students will have to figure it out and will respond at different times. Visual representation of the answer aids in memorization.) Have students stand in a circle. Say a child's name and toss him the ball. He catches the ball (or picks it up if he is unable to catch it) and then reads the math fact, word, letter, etc., that is closest to his right thumb. He then throws the ball to a student who hasn't had a turn yet and sits down. The last child to catch the ball throws it back to you.

VARIATIONS

You can also prepare a beach ball with pieces of information that require students to provide an answer. So if, for example, a student's right thumb lands next to or on "happy," you may ask for a synonym, such as "joyful." Other possibilities include antonyms or states and capitals.

Kings & Queens

MATERIALS

- Thick erasable marker
- Laminated inside-out birthday crowns (handmade or purchased)

CONTENT SUGGESTIONS

High-frequency words, spelling words, math facts, number recognition (to 1,000), coin identification (front and back), shapes (simple and complex), colors

HOW TO DO IT

Write one piece of your focus content on each crown, being sure to make all the crowns different. (Your students can help you with this.) Place one crown on each student's head and divide students into two groups facing each other. Have them sit down. A member of one group stands up, and the other group reads what is on her crown out loud. She sits down. A member of the other group stands up, and the opposite group reads what is on his crown. The groups repeat this process until every king or queen has had a chance to stand up. Once the rotation is complete, have students switch crowns and do it again, or have them erase their crowns so the crowns are ready for the next time.

VARIATION

Divide students into two groups. One group forms a small circle facing out, and the other group forms a larger circle around the first group facing in. On your cue, the members of each royal pair read each other's crowns. Students in the inner circle then take one step to the right, and the new pairs repeat the process. This continues until the students meet up with their original partners.

Lights, Cameras, Action

MATERIALS
- Magnetic tape
- 8 x 10-inch or larger picture frame (You can make the frame out of paper or use an actual frame.)
- Marker
- 4 x 6-inch index cards
- Student-made pretend cameras, optional (Animal cracker boxes painted black and silver make great pretend cameras.)

CONTENT SUGGESTIONS
High-frequency words, math facts, number recognition (to 1,000), shapes (simple and complex), coin identification (front and back), word families, fluency phrases

HOW TO DO IT
Affix magnetic tape to the back of the picture frame and attach the frame to your chalkboard if the board is magnetic or to a large baking sheet if it's not. Write your desired content on index cards and affix a piece of magnetic tape to the back of each card. Have students take out their "cameras" and face the frame. If they did not make cameras, they can use their hands to pretend they are taking pictures. Place an index card inside the frame. Have students read it out loud and then say "Click" to take a picture of the card. Place a new card in the frame and repeat the process.

VARIATION

If you want to focus on spelling words, follow the same procedure, but have students say the word, spell it, say it again, and then say "Click."

Say What?

MATERIALS
- Marker
- 4 x 6-inch index cards

CONTENT SUGGESTIONS
Spelling words, math facts, high-frequency words, letter recognition, word families

HOW TO DO IT

Write your focus content on index cards. Show students how to cover their teeth with their lips (to make them appear as if they had only gums in their mouths) and let them practice talking like this. Then show them an index card and let them read or spell what's written on it using their newfound speaking technique. Challenge them not to smile while they are talking in this special way. Review as much of the content as time allows. If you want to reinforce something on an index card, you can say "Say what?" and have students repeat it for even more practice and fun.

VARIATION

Have students practice reading tongue twisters that contain a focus letter or word family while keeping their lips over their teeth. It's very funny!

Boom Whackers

MATERIALS
♦ Marker
♦ 4 x 6-inch index cards
♦ 2 items per student that can be tapped together: music sticks, castanets, triangles and strikers, wooden dowels or blocks

CONTENT SUGGESTIONS
Spelling words, skip counting (2s, 5s, 10s, 25s, 50s, 100s, 1,000s), math facts, backward counting, syllable counting, months of the year, days of the week, alphabet sequence

HOW TO DO IT
Write your focus content on index cards. Place a card where everyone can see it. Have students say what's on the card, tap out each part (each letter of a word, each segment of a math fact, etc.) with their noisemakers, and then say what's on the card again. If you are doing a sequential drill such as reciting numbers in order or the months of the year, simply have students tap their noisemakers together each time they speak.

VARIATIONS
Students can march in place, clap their hands, or drum on their desks with their hands while reciting the information. (A footstep, clap, or tap represents each number, letter, etc.) You can also make pom-poms for each student and have them cheer or chant the information.

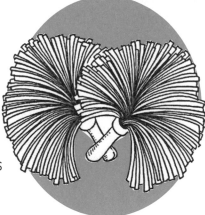

Land Ho!

MATERIALS
- Marker
- 4 x 6-inch index cards
- Paper towel tube for each student

CONTENT SUGGESTIONS
High-frequency words, word families, blend/digraph sounds, number recognition (to 1,000), shapes (simple and complex), colors, coin identification (front and back), math facts

HOW TO DO IT

Write the appropriate content on index cards. Supply each student with a paper towel tube (have students decorate their tubes, if desired) and tell them that they will be skill explorers, just like Christopher Columbus and Ferdinand Magellan were world explorers. Show students how to use their "looking glasses." Post an index card where everyone can see it. Have students read it while looking through their tubes and repeating the words "Land ho! I see _____" (a rectangle, 482, etc.). Post another card and continue the exploration.

VARIATION

Make binoculars! Cut each paper towel tube in half and glue the pieces together in the center. Make a hole in each tube, thread a string through each side, and tie the strings together in the back so the binoculars can be worn around the neck. (You or your students can do this, depending on their age.) Have students scout out the content as described above. You may tell them to pretend that they're bird-watchers instead of explorers and to say "Shh! I see a rare yellow-bellied _____."

ALSO BY LAUREEN REYNOLDS

Centers Made Simple
Hyperactive Students Are Never Absent (with Char Forsten, Jim Grant, and
    Betty Hollas)
Poems for Math Practice
Poems for Sight-Word Practice
Poems for Word-Family Practice

> Bring Laureen Reynolds right to your school
> for on-site training!
> To learn how, call (877) 388-2054.